INTENTIONAL MEANDERING

THROUGH THE *Lord's Prayer*

A MEDITATIVE JOURNEY WITH JESUS

INTENTIONAL MEANDERING

THROUGH THE Lord's Prayer

A MEDITATIVE JOURNEY WITH JESUS

Bill Ryan

Recorded Meditations by Bill Ryan
Illustrated by Julian Ryan
Music by Cory Ryan
Cover by Chad McElwain

This book or parts thereof may not be reproduced in any form, stored in a retrieval system or transmitted in any form by any means:--electronic, mechanical, photocopy, recording, or otherwise--without prior written permission of the author except as provided by United States of America copyright law.

Unless otherwise noted, all Scripture quotations are from the New King James Version of the Bible. Copyright © 1979, 1980, 1982 by Thomas Nelson Inc., publishers. Used by permission.

Scriptures taken from the Holy Bible, New International Version®, NIV®. Copyright © 1973, 1978, 1984, 2011 by Biblica, Inc.™ Used by permission of Zondervan. All rights reserved worldwide. www.zondervan.com The "NIV" and "New International Version" are trademarks registered in the United States Patent and Trademark Office by Biblica, Inc.™

Scripture taken from The Message. Copyright © 1993, 1994, 1995, 1996, 2000, 2001, 2002. Used by permission of NavPress Publishing Group.

Scripture quotations marked (NLT) are taken from the Holy Bible, New Living Translation, copyright © 1996, 2004, 2007 by Tyndale House Foundation. Used by permission of Tyndale House Publishers, Inc., Carol Stream, IL 60188. All rights reserved.

Scripture quotations are from The Holy Bible, English Standard Version® (ESV®), copyright © 2001 by Crossway, a publishing ministry of Good News Publishers. Used by permission. All rights reserved.

Scripture quotations taken from the (NASB®) New American Standard Bible®, Copyright © 1960, 1971, 1977, 1995, 2020 by The Lockman Foundation. Used by permission. All rights reserved. www.lockman.org

Copyright © 2023 by William Harvey Ryan
All rights reserved.

Recorded Meditations by Bill Ryan

Illustrations by Julian Ryan

Music by Cory Ryan

Cover and Book Design by Chad McElwain

Visit the author's website at www.intentionalmeandering.com

While the author has made every effort to provide accurate internet addresses at the time of publication, neither the publisher nor the author assumes any responsibility for error or for changes that occur after publication.

Dedication

(From and) To the Father
Through Jesus
By the Holy Spirit

Thank you for first loving me.

Bill Ryan

Contents

Preface
  A Word from Your Fellow Pathfinder . . . . **xv**

Chapter 1
  Preparing for Prayer:
  En Route to the Trailhead 21

Chapter 2
  The Lords Prayer:
  The Trail Master's Directions 35
  Introduction to Meandering with Friends 37

Chapter 3
  A Fellow Pathfinder Shares His Notes:
  A Friend on the Trail 41

Chapter 4
  Explore your Unique Paths 85

Acknowledgements 123

About the Authors 124

Why I Wrote This Book

Our fraternity inducted a new pledge who had written and published a book that made the New York Times Best Seller List when he was 18. I asked him if he had written the book with the intent of commercial success. He responded, "No, I wrote it because I had to." He was driven to capture an inspiration.

In short, he couldn't not write the book.

That's my story. I began the practice of praying through the Lord's Prayer about 40 years ago. The insights became deeper and wider and more exciting. I began to record them so that I wouldn't forget. My wife and I had children... then grandchildren, and I wanted to share the adventure with them. Meanwhile, our pastor shared my early notes with the congregation. The response was encouraging. I offered the concept and some of the content in Bible studies, small groups and speaking engagements, and people used terms like "Life changing".

By now, I knew I was writing a book, maybe even for publication. Intentional Meandering continued to grow (and continues to this day). New insights and inspirations are routine. That's the beauty. When you pray from the foundation that Jesus gave you, your prayer life becomes living and breathing.

I'm excited to share, not just the content, but the process. My prayer is that you will know the intimate love and person of Jesus through the Holy Spirit's leading in your own journey. My prayer is that you will look forward to prayer, record your own notes, and maybe write a best seller.

People have asked me about my goals for this book. Whereas, I am a habitual goal setter, I have no metrics. I can simply identify the mission, which is the mission for my life: "Love God Contagiously."

I pray that you catch the love,

Bill

Many chapters have a link to a short meditation directed by the author. All meditations can be found on the website: **intentionalmeandering.com**.

Consider using the meditations to help you
Be Present Not Tense.

About QR Codes

1. Using your mobile device, open your camera app and point your camera at the QR code. *(Like the one to the left.)*

2 . When your camera scans the QR code, you'll see an icon or web address on your screen near the code.

3. You'll go to the associated website via your phone's web browser, which should launch automatically.

(The QR code on the previous page should direct you to intentionalmeandering.com.)

Cory Ryan composed and recorded
an original score of **The Lord's Prayer**.

ILLUSTRATION BY **JULIAN RYAN**

Preface

A Word from Your Fellow Pathfinder

"He has shown you, O mortal, what is good. And what does the Lord require of you? To act justly and to love mercy and to walk humbly with your God."
- Micah 6:8 NIV

"Not all those who wander are lost."
- J.R.R. Tolkien

"Oh, the places you'll go!"
- Dr. Seuss

Are you bored with prayer?
Are you boring in prayer?
Is the thrill gone...or never was?

Can you relate to:

What do I say to the invisible Creator of the Universe?

Is he everywhere, including always right here with me, eager to listen and inspire?

Does he know everything about everything and everyone, including me? Is my prayer redundant?

Does he know me better than I know myself? Does he know what's good for me better than I do?

Is prayer something God just wants me to check off my to-do list every day, or does he want quality time in a mutually passionate relationship?

Does God intend for our relationship to be this difficult? If so, why?

My journey with Jesus and his prescribed "Lord's Prayer" has transformed my relationship with God. My daily walk with Jesus, guided by the Holy Spirit, is a conversation with a friend I love and who loves me.

It's fun. It's joyful.
It's expert guidance, vital instruction.
It's resurrecting. It's abundant life.
It's transparent and transformative.
It's an adventure.
It's a dance or a skip or a slogging, challenging trek.
It's a stroll down a familiar path or a free-spirited exploration of alluring terrain.

This path is not the only way to pray. In fact, it's not the only way Jesus prayed.

But it is my favorite way to start a day. It is *not* a quick recitation speed talk check-off, but an intentional slowing, a leisurely hand-in-hand stroll. It initiates a time with the Creator of the Universe that inspires and energizes *praying without ceasing* throughout the day.

I am disciplined, but I'm not inflexible in starting my day in intimate conversation with God. Sometimes I just listen for God's voice in silence, or pray Scriptures, or sing songs of praise and worship. Worship music can usher you into that simultaneous sense of reverent awe and trusting serenity. As you meander through this book, you will find some QR codes that will lead you to music and meditations.

When I do start by praying the way Jesus taught us to pray, my day is perceptibly better. The prayer is not some magic chant that removes all challenges and obstacles. It simply invites the Holy Spirit to take charge of my life, and he does. PRAYER CHANGES ME, the way I perceive things, the way I react...and proact. It gives me a lens of love and truth through which I see the world and respond.

Intentional Meandering is not intended to add to the Bible. The Bible is the perfect document, living and breathing. This book reflects my experience in going deeper in meditation and relationship. It is not a prescription, but it is a demonstration and, hopefully, a catalyst. It is an invitation to walk and explore The Lord's Prayer with Jesus, and let the Holy Spirit take you on some delightful, mysterious trails.

Intentional Meandering is not a page flipper, a one-sit read. Set it down and reflect. Listen. Jot some notes. My prayer is that you spend more time in reflection than in reading.

Be transformed by the renewing of your mind.

Walk with God.
Explore with God.
Meander with God.

Enjoy his company.

***Alert:** If you embrace this practice, The Lord's Prayer may become a new and different experience. You will likely settle into a slower, more contemplative approach. You may find yourself silently protesting, even resenting, any attempts to rush you through a mass rote oration.

**MEDITATION
INTRODUCTION**

intentionalmeandering.com/meditations/introduction

How to Use This Book

- Read it slowly.
- Savor it.
- Spend time listening to the prompting of the Holy Spirit.
- Give the content time to filter from your head to your heart.
- Walk step-for-step with the Holy Spirit, not lagging behind and not forging ahead.

You don't have to read this book. It's a "Get to" and a "Want to", rather than a "Have to".

This is a relationship, not a transaction.

God is always speaking to you. As your relationship gets more intimate, and you turn your ear to him, he speaks with you.

As you focus on him, he might speak with you through the pages of this book.

ILLUSTRATION BY **JULIAN RYAN**

CHAPTER 1

Preparing for Prayer
En Route to the Trailhead

Relationship

Before you launch into prayer, picture your relationship with God the Father.

You go to meet with your Father to take a walk together. As you enter his throne room, you are awed by his majesty and glory. You can't speak and you drop to your knees. You crawl to the foot of his throne. You feel a comforting, familiar hand on your shoulder.

It's Jesus. He picks you up. You are still awestruck, but you have never felt more secure and more loved in your life.

You are home.

Know that God created you for intimate conversation with him. He loves you and your discussions.

He hears you and he responds.

Get Real with God

Bring both boldness and humility to this authentic relationship. Share what's on your mind. Be transparent. Be vulnerable. You might as well. He already knows.

Ask

I've missed what could have been close relationships because I didn't initiate. Sometimes I didn't even respond.

God wants you to reach out. He wants you to respond. He wants you to be humble, but he also wants you to be bold. He wants a real relationship. God wants to hear what's on your mind.

Tell him.

> *Jesus' disciple, James, wrote "You do not have, because you do not ask God."*
> - James 4:2b ESV

Seek to Align Your Imperfect Will with God's Perfect Will

God loves me, but he doesn't give me unlimited power to squander or destroy myself and others.

I've learned that God's response to my prayer is not quite as simple as inserting a dollar into a prayer vending machine and out pops my selection every time.

Faith is a prerequisite to your pursuing God in prayer. Like any good relationship, you will want to know about him and what he wants. You will seek to align your prayers with his will and what pleases him.

Prayer is powerful. God is all- powerful. It is in your best interest to recognize that he sees and directs the whole picture.

He always hears you. He always answers your prayers. He often surprises you with his answers. When you are truly aligned, you understand that He is God, you are not, and that is best. Then you will be grateful, whether his answer is "Yes", "No", or "Not now".

> *Jesus told us, "I tell you the truth, anyone who believes in me will do the same works I have done, and even greater works, because I am going to be with the Father. You can ask for anything in my name, and I will do it, so that the Son can bring glory to the Father. Yes, ask me for anything in my name, and I will do it!"*
> - John 14:12-14 NLT

Believe

> *Jesus told us, "Truly I tell you, if you have faith and don't doubt... you can say to this mountain, 'Go, throw yourself into the sea,' and it will be done. If you believe, you will receive whatever you ask for in prayer."*
> - Matthew 21:21-22 NIV

I have struggled with belief. I have also found that, the more I believe, the more God gives me reasons to believe in personal experiences and intellectual rationale.

Trust

> Breathe deep and easy.
> Relax.
> You are safe. You can trust him.
> Let go.
> You don't need to control. You don't have to. Let him.

BE STILL AND KNOW THAT I AM GOD

BE STILL AND KNOW THAT I AM

BE STILL AND KNOW

BE STILL

BE

Attributes of a Friend

I've been learning how to be a true friend for 75 years. It's a work in process.

I've been learning that God is my best friend, and that I'm a better friend to others when I embrace friendship with him.

Friendship is a dance. It's dating. It's learning how to best relate to your friend. That will always be a work in process.

Father God made me, and you, on purpose, in his image, for an intimate relationship with him, now and for eternity.

You can be in awe of him and a close friend at the same time.

How do you relate to a close friend?

How do you expect them to relate to you? How do you communicate with an intimate friend?

How do you communicate with God?

Here are some general questions on friendship that might inspire epiphanies on your friendship with God:

- Do you talk *at* a friend? Do you talk *to* a friend? Or do you have discussion *with* your friend?
- Is friendship unilateral or bilateral?
- Is friendship a give or a get or both?
- Are you honest, transparent, and vulnerable with each other, even when it's uncomfortable? Are you trusting and trustworthy?
- Are you dependable? Is your friend dependable?
- Are you loyal?
- Are you both helpful and supportive in good times and bad times?
- Are you protective of each other? Do you stand up for each other?
- Are you mutually kind and compassionate?
- Are you mutually self-sacrificial, or is your relationship a cost/benefit transaction?
- Do you invest time and resources in your relationship without keeping score?
- Are you persistent in sustaining your relationship?
- Do you dare to engage in deep, meaningful conversations? Do you collaborate in pursuit of truth and love?
- Are you comfortable with silence?
- Do you make each other laugh? Do you have fun together?
- Do you enjoy shared interests?
- Are you excited to be in each other's company? Are

you truly present?
- Are you intentional and spontaneous in your friendship?
- Do you actively listen to each other? Do you seek first to understand, then be understood?
- Do you celebrate each other's successes?
- Are you forgiving? Do you cut each other slack?

How do your answers describe your close relationships?

How do they describe your relationship with God?

Listening Skills

One of the attributes of a friend is to be a good listener. Again, praying, at its best, is not talking at God or to God. It is talking with God. That entails listening.

"This is my Son, my Chosen One. Listen to him."
- Luke 9:35 NASB

I spent a lot of my life seeking to tell my story and impress others. I devoted myself to be recognized as an achiever and earn the approval of others.

It's taken me many decades to acquire a passion to hear everyone else's story.

Everyone is precious.
Everyone has a story.
The best use of my stories is to encourage others to tell there's.
God has stories.

What are the characteristics of a good listener,

whether you are in human company or divine?

- Focus on the other person.

  - No multi-tasking or competing media.
  - Encourage them to tell their story.
  - Be geninely interested in them.
  - Be present.

- Engage in active listening.

  - Ask clarifying questions.
  - Repeat what you hear them say, or what you think they said.
  - Ask probing questions for deeper understanding.
  - Empathize. Listen for feelings and emotions, as well as content. Ask them what they are feeling.
  - Find comfort and encourage dialogue with silence.
  - Take notes, if appropriate, during or following conversation, for future reference.

God's Presence

There have been times in my life when I avoided God. I didn't really know him, but I was pretty sure that, whoever he was, he didn't approve of what I was thinking and doing.

Psalm 139 confirmed my concerns.

God flipped the paradigm. He framed all of his presence and power in his perfect, infinite, eternal, and unconditional love for me. Rather than feeling threatened and claustrophobic and violated, I felt love and peace and joy and purpose and hope.

> *You have searched me, Lord, and you know me. You know when I sit and when I rise; you perceive my thoughts from afar. You discern my going out and my lying down; you*

are familiar with all my ways. Before a word is on my tongue, you, Lord, know it completely. You hem me in behind and before, and you lay your hand upon me. Such knowledge is too wonderful for me, too lofty for me to attain. Where can I go from your Spirit? Where can I flee from your presence?
- Psalm 139:1-7 NIV

How do you feel about omnipresent, omniscient, omnipotent God searching you, knowing you, and leading you?

Do you feel hemmed in or liberated? Is his imminent intimate presence too wonderful for you?

Do you want to rest *with* him or flee *from* him?

Are his thoughts precious to you?

Do you want his benevolent and faithful guidance and direction? Are you willing to submit?

What insights do you get from your answers to these questions?

Christ Be With Me
Christ with me, Christ before me, Christ behind me,
Christ in me, Christ beneath me, Christ above me,
Christ on my right, Christ on my left,
Christ where I lie, Christ where I sit, Christ where I arise,
Christ in the heart of everyone who thinks of me,
Christ in the mouth of every one who speaks to me,
Christ in every eye that sees me,
Christ in every ear that hears me.
Salvation is of the Lord.
Salvation is of the Christ.
May your salvation, Lord, be ever with us.
- Saint Patrick

Intentional Spontaneity

Do you plan your interactions with other people or do you go with the flow? Do you follow a carefully orchestrated strategy or do you call audibles as plays unfold? Do you do some of both?

Have a prayer plan, but be open to off-trail explorations and inspirations.

Ask the Holy Spirit where he wants you to go in your prayer. Seek to align your will with God's will.

> *In the same way, the Spirit helps us in our weakness. We do not know what we ought to pray for, but the Spirit himself intercedes for us with wordless groans. And he who searches our hearts knows the mind of the Spirit, because the Spirit intercedes for God's people in accordance with the will of God.*
> - Romans 8:26-27 NIV

"Praying without ceasing" means going to God with anything, anytime, anywhere. But you will find that a set time and place every day that is free from distractions will engage your subconscious and inspire you to pray throughout your day.

- A quiet place with no distractions, no disruptions, no multitasking.
- Have your Bible handy. As you and Jesus ("The Word") are having words, he may direct you to the written Word.
- Keep a prayer journal within reach to record your thoughts. You concentrate better if you aren't struggling to remember an epiphany. Date your entries and reread them to sustain your intercessory prayers and celebrate God's answers.
- Remove any obstacles of unconfessed, unrepentant sin against God and others. Ask forgiveness. Offer forgiveness. Forgive yourself.
- Find an optimal *pace* for you and God to converse.

Too slow and you get distracted or fall asleep. Too fast and it's a transaction, rather than a relationship. Step-for-step with the Holy Spirit, not racing ahead or lagging behind.
- If you miss prayer time, be convicted but not condemned. God still wants to meet with you. Refresh your relationship when you can. If you get distracted, gently find your way back.
- Try praying on your knees with your eyes closed. Pray with your hands clasped, hands open, arms folded across your chest or reaching up. Pray prostrate, face down arms and legs outstretched. Pray sitting up or reclining. Pray eyes open while you are engaged in your day.
- Pray spontaneously and perpetually, before, during, and between challenges and opportunities that arise. Pray in bed. Pray when you garden, when you drive, when you eat, when you work or study, when you rest, when you meet with others, when you sing in the shower. Pray when you bicycle, when you swim, when you do chores, when you…
- Pray when you walk your neighborhood. Intercede for your neighbors with prayer.
- Find peace in the quiet of a forest or focus on God and his precious people in the rush of a crowded city street or an airport.

Attitude of Gratitude

Gratefulness releases oxytocin (the "love hormone") in the giver and the receiver. It can lower your blood pressure, improve your immune response, mental health, *and relationships.*

You have reason to be grateful: The Creator of the Universe craves your company.

Momentary happiness hinges on immediate circumstances: "I want what I want when I want it!" On the other hand, lasting joy is dependent on *this one circumstance*: "I love Jesus. Jesus loves me."

Your attitude of gratitude starts with intentional moments of appreciation, which become an enduring, eternal spontaneity.

- Give thanks for another day of life and love when you wake. Try it before you arise and just after you arise to see which works best for you. Pray before you engage with the world via TV, newspaper, or social media.
- Give thanks when you eat breakfast and when you head to work or school.
- Give thanks for every challenge, every learning opportunity, every ministry opportunity. Give thanks for pleasures and even for suffering.

Count it all joy, my brothers, when you meet trials of various kinds...
- James 1:2 ESV

- Give thanks for breakfast, lunch, and dinner.
- Give thanks for safe travel home.
- Give thanks for exercise.
- Give thanks for shelter.
- At the beginning of a family meal, offer each person an opportunity to express their gratefulness for something or someone.
- Give thanks for family and friends by name.
- Give thanks for the day in retrospect.
- Give thanks for rest, and ask that the rest equips you to love and serve again tomorrow.

NOTES

SCAN CODE

intentionalmeandering.com/meditations/hold-me

MEDITATION AND MUSIC
HOLD ME

NOTES

ILLUSTRATION BY **JULIAN RYAN**

CHAPTER 2

The Lord's Prayer
The Trail Master's Directions

This, then, is how you should pray:
Our Father, who art in heaven, hallowed be thy name.
Thy Kingdom come, thy will be done, on earth as it is in
heaven. Give us this day our daily bread, and forgive us
our trespasses, as we forgive those who trespass against
us. And lead us not into temptation, but deliver us from
evil, for thine is the Kingdom, and the power, and the
glory forever, Amen.
- Matthew 6:9-13
   Traditional Ecumenical Version

After this manner therefore pray ye:
Our Father which art in heaven,
Hallowed be thy name.
Thy kingdom come, thy will be done in earth as it is in
heaven.
Give us this day our daily bread.
And forgive us our debts, as we forgive our debtors.
And lead us not into temptation, but deliver us from evil.
For thine is the kingdom, and the power, and the glory,
forever. Amen.
- Matthew 6:9-13
   King James Version

And when you come before God, don't turn that into a theatrical production either. All these people making a regular show out of their prayers, hoping for fifteen minutes of fame! Do you think God sits in a box seat?

Here's what I want you to do: Find a quiet, secluded place so you won't be tempted to role-play before God. Just be there as simply and honestly as you can manage. The focus will shift from you to God, and you will begin to sense his grace... This is your Father you are dealing with, and he knows better than you what you need.
With a God like this loving you, you can pray very simply. Like this:

> *Our Father in heaven,*
> *Reveal who you are.*
> *Set the world right;*
> *Do what's best –*
>   *as above, so below.*
> *Keep us alive with three square meals.*
> *Keep us forgiven with you and forgiving others.*
> *Keep us safe from ourselves and the Devil.*
> *You're in charge!*
> *You can do anything you want!*
> *You're ablaze in beauty!*
>   *Yes. Yes. Yes.*

- Matthew 6:8-13

  The Message

Initiating Your Stroll with Friends

"If I had a flower for every time I thought of you...I could walk through my garden forever."
- Alfred Tennyson

    The mission of this book is to give you an on-ramp to your own discussions with God. The format is designed to show you the main trail, then guide you on some of the paths that have inspired my journey, then encourage you to find your own trails.

    The Lord's Prayer is divided into nine sections. Chapter 3 offers the primary text, followed by my basic framework for daily prayer. You and I walk together with Jesus.

    My inspirations are not prescriptive. They are intended to inspire you to follow the Holy Spirit to find your own way at your own pace.

    In Chapter 4 you are accompanied solely by the Holy Spirit (unless you invite others to join you). You have prompts to urge you off the beaten path, and space to take notes. I pray that the space is insufficient. As you embark on this adventure, the Spirit will give you your own prompts.

    You will always have at least one friend on this journey.

NOTES

ILLUSTRATION BY **JULIAN RYAN**

CHAPTER 3

A Fellow Pathfinder Shares His Notes
A Friend on The Trail

Our Father Who art in Heaven

Heavenly Father

Creator,

Provider,

Protector,

Comforter,

Counsellor,

Loving Disciplinarian,

Teacher,

Coach,

Encourager,

Inspiration,

Role Model...

NOTES

SCAN CODE

intentionalmeandering.com/meditations/our-father

MEDITATION
OUR FATHER

NOTES

Hallowed be Thy Name

Lord, you alone are Holy.

You define, model and inspire "Holy" and "Righteous".

You alone are perfect love, perfect truth, perfect justice, perfect grace and perfect mercy.

You alone are infinite love, infinite truth, infinite justice, infinite grace and infinite mercy.

You alone are eternal love, eternal truth, eternal justice, eternal grace and eternal mercy.

You alone are unconditional love, unconditional truth, unconditional justice.

Unconditional grace, and *mercy upon humble request.*

> You alone are omnipresent:
>
> - You are here.
> - You are there.
> - You are everywhere, always.
> - With everyone, with me right now.
> - You never leave me.
>   Your presence is comforting to me, and I trust you.
>
> You alone are omniscient:
>
> - You know everything about everything and everyone.
> - You know me better than I know myself.
> - You know what's good for me.
> - You know what to do. Your infinite knowledge gives me confidence in you, and I trust you.

You alone are omnipotent:

- You can do it.
- There are no obstacles or forces that you cannot overcome. I can rely on your ultimate power, applied perfectly.
- With you, all things are possible.
- You are able and *I trust you*.

You alone are benevolent:

- You think it and do it in love.
- Love is the engine and the Engineer.
- You care for me and *I trust you*.

You alone are faithful:

- You keep all of your promises all the time.
- You never forsake me.
- *I trust you*.

Lord, you alone are God, worthy of worship and adoration and I do worship and adore you.

I am in love with you.

I am in awe of you, sitting on your throne, even as you welcome me into your lap.

I submit my life, this moment, and all moments to you.

NOTES

MEDITATION
HOLY IS YOUR NAME

intentionalmeandering.com/meditations/holy-is-your-name

NOTES

\|/

Thy Kingdom come, thy will be done, on Earth as it is in Heaven

Lord, thy kingdom come, thy will be done.

In me:

- May I live to serve and glorify you.
- Change my heart, hence my acts; conform them to your perfect will.
- Empty me of myself and fill me with you.

In my family:

- In our love for each other and for you, our relationships and ministries to others and to you, our health, our work and finances, our fun and laughter together.

In my extended family, friends, strangers and enemies (by name, and also people I don't yet know and might meet today):

- May we all know you personally as our Lord and our Savior. May we all live together in heaven with each other and with you. Give us the awareness, the love and the actions to introduce others to you, today and all days, for now and for eternity.

In my vocation, my business, and everyone I meet in that context.

In my church and in all of the churches that you call your bride, your "Big C" Church, and all of your parachurch ministries.

In our schools:

- Inspire the intent and the content of the instruction of our youth with your love and your truth.
- Translate knowledge to wisdom. Inspire all constituents to seek, recognize, and promote your absolute truth and demonstrate your love through students, parents, teachers and aides,

- coaches, directors, administrators, curriculum directors, counselors, secretaries, librarians, custodians, unions, school board and electorate, state and federal officials.
- Public, Private, Christian, Charter, Vocational, Homeschool and daily instruction at home.
- Preschool, middle school, high school, college, graduate, postgrad.

In our families:

- The primary institution, the foundation of society.

In our communities:

- Neighbors, employers and employees, faith institutions, voters, civil servants and elected leaders, caring and serving each other as "community".

In our cities and our states:

- Bless and give us the wisdom to seek your counsel.

In our nation:

- "One nation, under God, indivisible, with liberty and justice for all."
- Give us the character to seek your will and the best interests of others, to collaborate to be a force for good in the world.

In our world:

- On all of the earth as it is in heaven.

NOTES

MEDITATION
THY KINGDOM COME

intentionalmeandering.com/meditations/thy-kingdom-come

NOTES

Give us this day our daily bread

Lord, everything good that comes to us is from your generous hand.

Thank you.

May we be ever grateful and thankful to you for showering us with blessings, for
- life
- love
- talents
- motivations
- opportunities
- energies
- sustenance

> For Jesus Christ, our example, our teacher, our hero, our Savior and Lord.
>
> For the Holy Spirit, our guide, our inspiration.

May we be grateful for what you don't give us, as well as what you do give us, and for the valleys as well as the mountaintops.

May we be faithful stewards and effective ambassadors for you.

May we live to please and glorify you.

Lord, give us this day our...

> Physical daily bread:
> - food
> - clothing
> - shelter
> - rest
> - exercise
> - loving touch
> - health
> - athletic ability

Social / Emotional daily bread:
- Your love of relationships; your love, joy, peace, patience, kindness, goodness, faithfulness, gentleness and self-control; your transparency, vulnerability, humility, boldness, and sense of humor.

Intellectual daily bread:
- Stretch us.
- Give us your thoughts and your wisdom as we are capable of using them for you and your glory.

Spiritual daily bread:
- Give us life and love
    in,
    with,
    through,
    by,
    for,
    of,
    from, and
    to
    you.

NOTES

MEDITATION
GIVE US THIS DAY

intentionalmeandering.com/meditations/give-us-this-day

NOTES

Forgive us our trespasses...

Lord, I am... *sinful, self-centered and* full of *self-pride.*

I have willfully hurt
> you,
> others,
> and myself,
> by my disobedience,
> by omission and commision,
> and I'm sorry.

I try to justify and glorify myself by works and by lies.

I'm sorry for sins of pride, greed, fear, envy, lust, anger, gluttony, apathy and laziness.

I'm sorry for violating *all* of your Ten Commandments:

Other gods before you,
idolatry,
blasphemy,
violating the Sabbath,
dishonoring my parents,
murder,
adultery,
theft,
lying
and coveting.

> Lord, *I ask Your forgiveness.* I thank you for providing for my forgiveness through the sacrifice of Jesus on the Cross. Before I could ever know myself, you knew me, loved me anyway, and suffered and died for me. You love me now and you will love me forever.
>
> *Thank you for forgiving me*, for giving me access to your throne, and for waiting for me, sometimes in the cold, outside my closed door, always ready, always hoping to embrace me.

NOTES

MEDITATION
FORGIVE US

intentionalmeandering.com/meditations/forgive-us

NOTES

\\|/

...as we forgive those who trespass against us

Lord, *help me to forgive others* as you forgive me, with the love you so freely supply.

Help others to forgive me with that same love.

Help me to forgive *myself* with that same love.

Help others to forgive *themselves* with that same love.

Help us all to forgive and allow ourselves to be forgiven.

NOTES

MEDITATION
AS WE FORGIVE

intentionalmeandering.com/meditations/as-we-forgive

NOTES

Lead us not into temptation...

Lord, spare me that pain.

Spare me from inflicting that pain on others and on you.

Help me to recognize and avoid temptation.

And, when I'm confronted, help me to *flee* and/or *fight with the Sword of the Spirit, the Word of God.*

Help me to recognize and walk your path according to
    your direction, your will, and your strength.

ILLUSTRATION BY **JULIAN RYAN**

NOTES

MEDITATION
LEAD US NOT

intentionalmeandering.com/meditations/lead-us-not

NOTES

But deliver us from evil

INTENTIONAL MEANDERING   A Fellow Pathfinder Shares His Notes

Lord,

> *Fight the battles for us and*
> *fight the war.*

Without you, we are lost.

Behind you, we are victorious.

Be our *Commander-in-Chief*.

Be our *Hero*.

Be our *Bodyguard*.

Be our *Social/Emotional-Guard*.

Be our *Intellect-Guard*.

Be our *Soul and Spirit-Guard*.

Put Your *armor* on us

> Belt of Truth
> Breastplate of Righteousness
> Shoes that carry us to spread your Gospel of peace
> Shield of Faith
> Helmet of Salvation
> Sword of the Spirit

Plant a *hedge of protection* and build your *fortifications* around us.

Surround us with your *angels*.

And bathe us in your white *light of truth*.

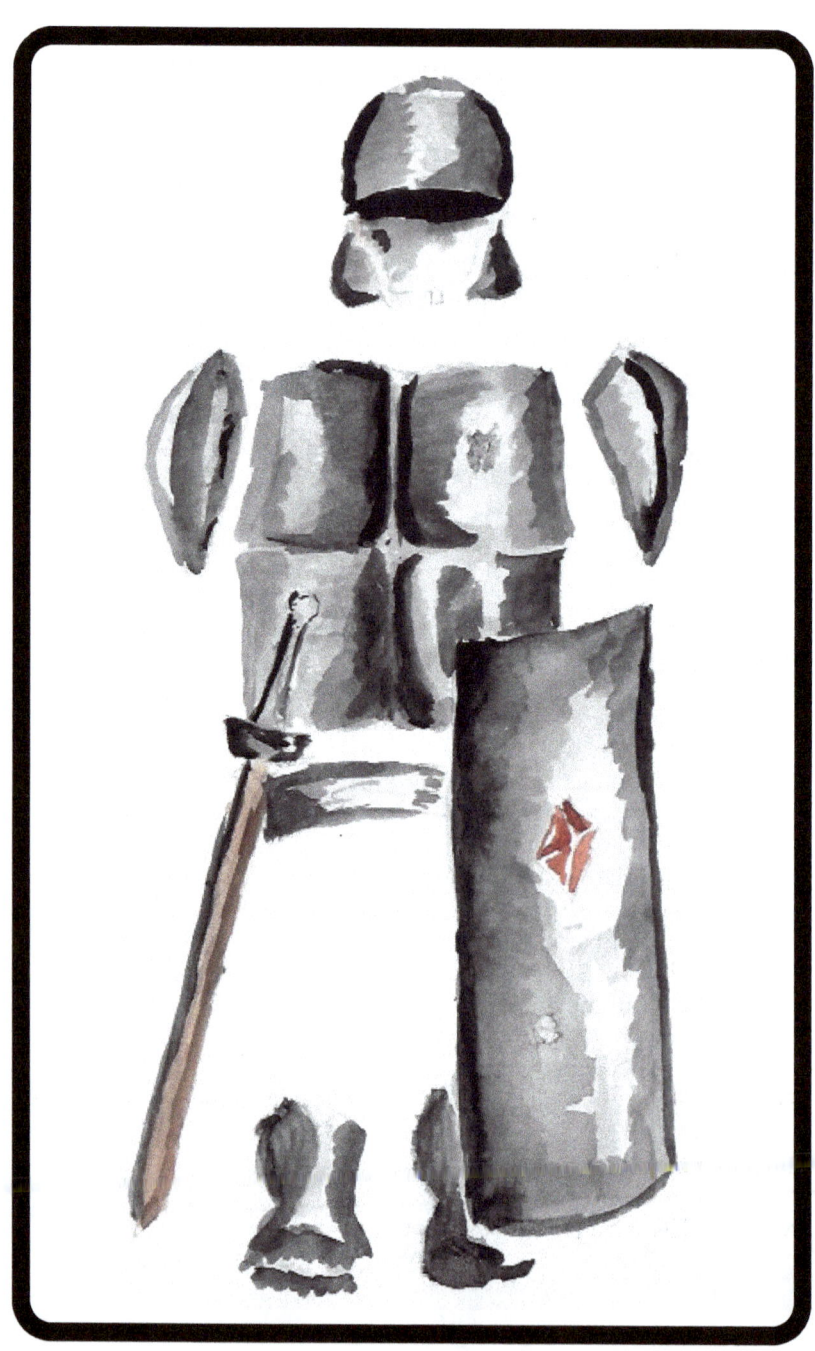

ILLUSTRATION BY **JULIAN RYAN**

NOTES

intentionalmeandering.com/meditations/deliver-us

MEDITATION
DELIVER US

NOTES

\\|/

**For Thine is the Kingdom
The Power
and The Glory
Forever
Amen**

For thine is the *righteous* **kingdom**...

The ***ultimate* power**...

And the ***rightful* glory**...

Forever.

Amen.

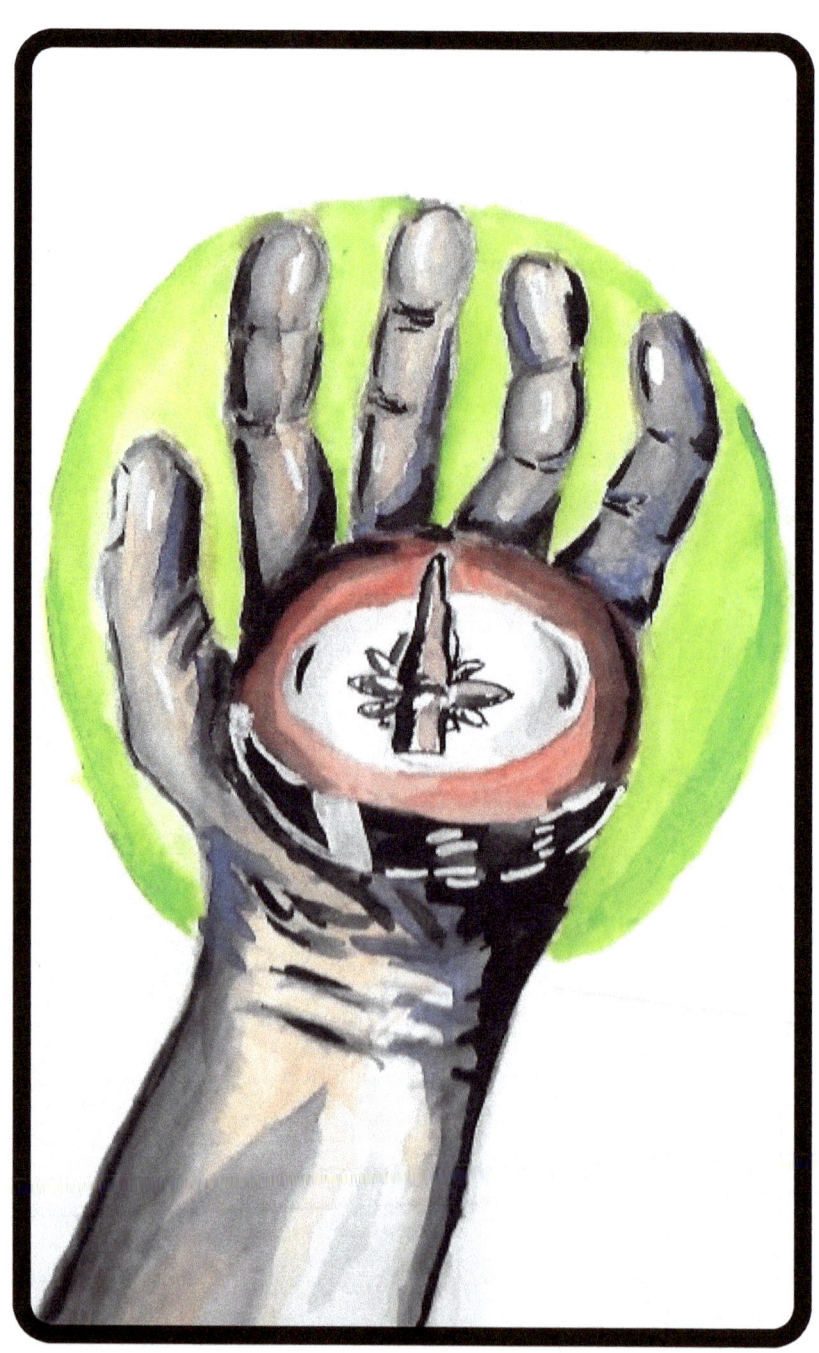

ILLUSTRATION BY **JULIAN RYAN**

CHAPTER 4

Exploring Your Unique Paths

The Lord's Prayer is again divided into nine sections. Each will offer the primary text, followed by questions to help you explore your unique paths. Record your creative experiences as you engage with the Creator in the spaces provided.

Our Father Who art in Heaven

Our Father, Who Art in Heaven

To whom does "Our" refer? Who is "Us"?

Who are we if God is our Father?

What are the characteristics of the ideal "Father"?

What is the response of a loving, grateful child?

The King James translation refers to the Father as "Which art in heaven". The Traditional Ecumenical translation uses "Who"? What pronoun do you prefer? Why?

"Art" refers to right now. Has it always referred to right now? Will it always? Does it refer to this present, this right now? When do you experience heaven? Do you have to wait until you die?

What is heaven? How does the Bible describe it? How would you describe it? Are you excited about the prospect of your eternity in heaven?

Where is heaven? Is it a specific geographical reference, or can you experience heaven in any space and time? Does the Father's address tell us something about Him and how we can best relate?

Why is there a heaven?

What do you think your role in heaven is/will be?

Hallowed be Thy name

Hallowed (Holy), be Thy name

Holy* means to be "set apart". How is God the Father set apart?

_____
_____
_____

Holy* means to be "perfect, transcendent, or spiritually pure, evoking adoration and reverence." How does this describe God?

_____
_____
_____

Holy* refers to the capacity to evoke "veneration or awe, being frightened beyond belief." How do you relate to being awed, terrified, and deeply in love with God and comforted by his presence?

_____
_____
_____

* Note: These definitions are from The Holman Bible Dictionary. God ultimately defines "Holy". We are, by nature, sinful. Yet he commands us to

> *"Be holy, because I am Holy"*
> - 1 Peter 1:16 HCSB
> - Leviticus 11:44-45, 19:2, ESV

Clearly, God has made provision for us to be holy.

Thy Kingdom come, thy will be done, on Earth as it is in Heaven

Thy Kingdom come, Thy will be done, on Earth as it is in Heaven

What is "Kingdom"?

- Territory subject to the dominion of a monarch.
- Population subject to a king.
- The power of supreme administration
- Heaven; State of glory in heaven

Paraphrased from KJV Dictionary Definition

Who governs a Kingdom? What is special about this Kingdom and this King?

What does it mean to invite a Kingdom to come in and take over? Take over what and who? How?

Do you want to be a subject of this King? Why? How do you submit?

What do you know about God's will? Can you trust his will? With your life? Do you want it to be done?

Do you want it here on earth? The same way it is in heaven?

Give us this day our daily bread

Give us this day our daily bread

Are you telling God or asking him? Does "Give us" mean we're entitled to command God? How do you prepare your heart for this request?

Who is "Us" and "Our"? For whom are you asking? Is it just you?

What is "bread"? Is it just a staple food, or does it include any form of nourishment? Is the nourishment physical only?

What is the time frame for the request? Are you asking God to supply your immediate needs, knowing that you can make the same request of your Father tomorrow, or do you want your storehouses full so that you can feel secure without him in the future?

How could God use you to supply other people's needs?

- Family, close friends
- Neighbors, community
- City, state
- Nation
- World

_____
_____
_____

ILLUSTRATION BY **JULIAN RYAN**

Forgive us our trespasses...

Forgive us our trespasses...

Who is "Us" and "Our"? Is this purely individual...or collective as well?

- What is the application to a family?
- A neighborhood?
- A community?
- A nation?
- The world?

What are trespasses? Have you been the victim of trespasses? Have you been guilty of trespassing?

What is the importance of humility? How is self-pride an obstacle?

What does it mean to forgive? Are you asking for a pardon or for the record to be expunged? Are you willing to offer that to others?

How do you *feel* when you are forgiven?

_____
_____
_____

How have you *responded* to someone who forgave you?

_____
_____
_____

\\|/

...as we forgive those who trespass against us

/|\

...as we forgive those who trespass against us

Do you really want to be judged by your own judgment standards?

Do you want justice or mercy for yourself? For others?

If full justice was applied to you, what would you get?

What do you get through God's mercy?

What are you prepared to offer to others?

Lead us not into temptation...

And lead us not into temptation

Are you prepared to follow God? To completely submit to him?

What tempts you? Who tempts you? Why? What is the attraction?

What experiences have you had with falling to temptation? What were the short-term benefits? What were the long-term consequences?

Do you think that you can get away with sin, that you can keep it hidden? Do you think that anyone ever gets away with sin?

How do you avoid temptation?

INTENTIONAL MEANDERING   Exploring Your Unique Paths

When you are tempted, how do you defend yourself? How do you prepare to flee or fight when confronted with temptation? When does your preparation begin for that time of trial?

_____
_____
_____

ILLUSTRATION BY **JULIAN RYAN**

But deliver us from evil

But deliver us from evil

What is evil? Who is evil?

What is your ability to defend yourself? What resources do you need?

What is your responsibility?

How has God delivered you when you were under attack?

How has God used you to help someone else when they were under attack?

ILLUSTRATION BY **JULIAN RYAN**

\\|/

**For Thine is the Kingdom
The Power
and The Glory
Forever
Amen**

For thine is the *righteous* kingdom, the *ultimate* power, and the *rightful* glory...

In what kind of kingdom do you choose to live and serve? Where do you find such a kingdom?

_____

_____

_____

How many ultimate absolutes are there? Do you want to *be* that power or *join and serve* it? What would your life and the world be like if you had that power?

_____

_____

_____

What would the world look like if *everyone* recognized God as God?

_____

_____

_____

What would the world look like if humans stopped trying to *be* God?

_____

_____

_____

Where is glory rightfully directed? On mortal, temporal, limited humans; on material possessions; or on immortal, eternal, infinite Creator God?

Forever

Was? Is? Will Be?

Amen

What does "Amen" mean? Do you believe what you have just offered in prayer?

In whose name can we go to God the Father with a prayer like this? With *any* prayer?

Who influences and inspires your prayer?

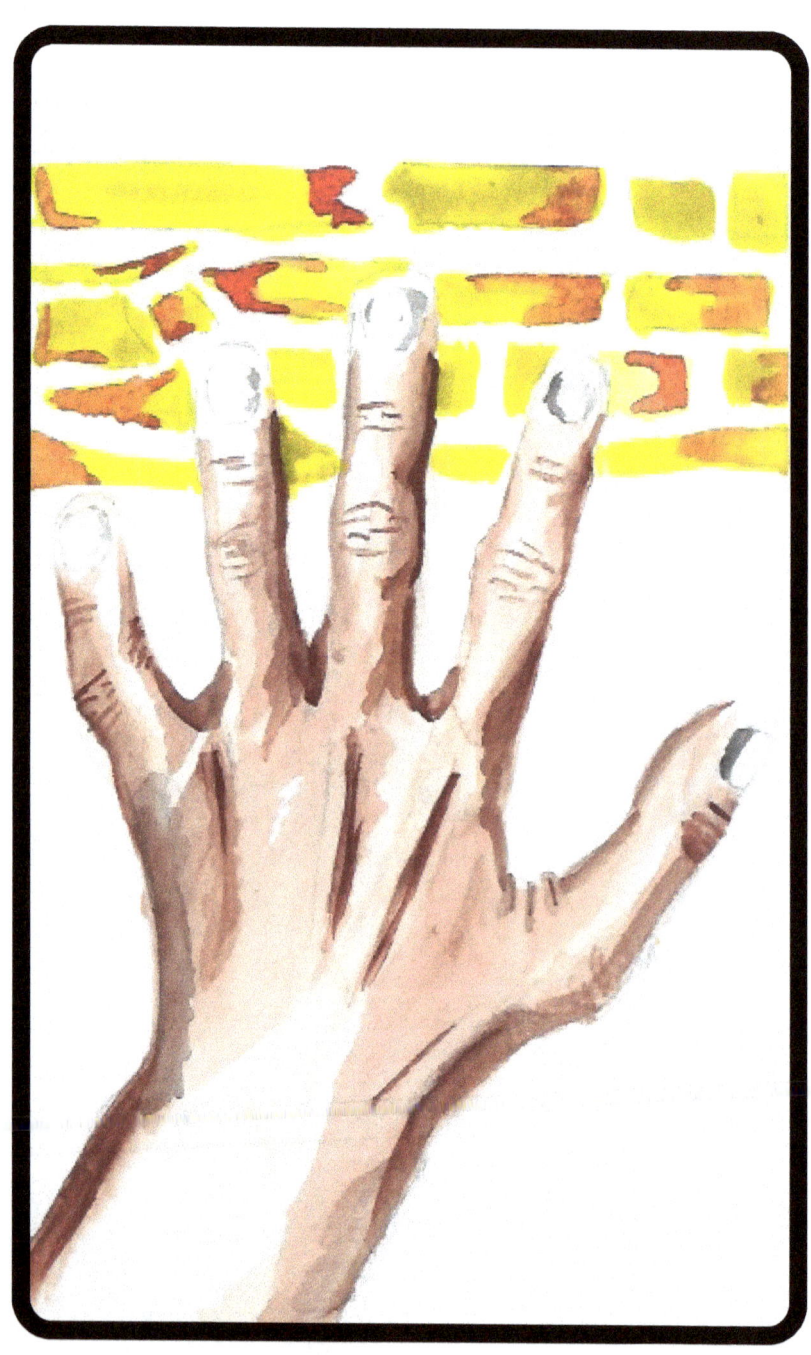

ILLUSTRATION BY **JULIAN RYAN**

Reverie Zone

Did you take the time to explore the Lord's prayer for yourself?

Your own quest will find paths I never walked.

Enjoy your travels.

Cory Ryan composed and recorded
an original score of **The Lord's Prayer**.

ILLUSTRATION BY **JULIAN RYAN**

Acknowledgements

Many thanks to God the Father for first loving me.

Many thanks to Jesus for living, dying, and living for me.

Many thanks to the Holy Spirit for giving me love to share and opportunities to share it.

Many thanks to my fellow pilgrims, a constant source of inspiration.

Many thanks to my wife, Vicki, and my daughter, Molly, conduits of God's love, who proofed, and formatted, and contributed valuable insights.

Many thanks to Julian for his extraordinary devotion to his artistic contribution.

Many thanks to my son Cory, my inspiring worship leader on Sundays and all days, for his musical contributions to this book.

Many thanks to my son-in-law, Alireza Yousefi, who engineered the narration and instrumental music to produce the meditations.

Many thanks to my publishing and marketing Sherpas, Chad McElwain, Shakerah McElwain and Brandy Alexander Wimberly.

Many thanks to all who took the time to read this work and to offer constructive suggestions and encouragement.

Who is Bill Ryan?

I was born to loving, nurturing parents. Consequently, I sometimes get it right as a loving, nurturing parent and grandparent.

I was born again when the Holy Spirit spoke through a college athlete I was coaching. He asked me whether I was a Christian, to which I answered "Yes." Then he asked me how I would answer God when he asks me why he should admit me to heaven. I offered a "Grade on the curve" answer, i.e., "I haven't killed anyone, tried to do the right thing, and I'm generally a nice guy (compared to others)." Rather than confront my theology, he invited me to read the book of John with him before practice the next day.

Epiphany! I realized that I had not known Jesus. I prayed to receive him as my Lord and Savior. I opened the gift and I am grateful.

In studying Jesus' exegesis on murder and adultery in Matthew 5, I'm convicted that I have violated all of the Ten Commandments. I realize the degree to which I am accountable...and forgiven. I am a sinner, saved by God's grace, and a work in process. At my best, I am a conduit of Jesus' love and truth.

I married a beautiful Christian girl, who has shown me how to love every day for over 50 years.

I am blessed by Christian friends who help me understand the Bible and grow in my relationship with the Father, the Son, and the Holy Spirit. Iron sharpens iron.

The Holy Spirit gives me insights and opportunities to serve, and the strength and resources to follow through.

I am grateful.

Now in my 70's, some would use the word "Retired" to describe my station in life. Those close to me would say that I'm working full time, just not getting paid. I am a writer and a speaker.

I am an athlete, transformed to see the fun and collaboration in competition.

I am an entrepreneur. God started, grew, then sold the business he gave me to found and lead.

I am blessed by insightful mentors, and I pay it forward at every opportunity.

I have learned that, whether in athletics, business, or chance meetings, I am surrounded by platforms for ministry.

I am grateful.

INTENTIONAL MEANDERING

THROUGH THE *Lord's Prayer*

A MEDITATIVE JOURNEY WITH JESUS

Who is Julian Ryan?

Julian is my grandson.

He is a scholar, an athlete, a reader, and he plays a good game of chess. He is an artist, with a heart and soul to serve. He is a man after God's heart.

He is not waiting for "Half Time" to figure out how to live a life of significance.

He is a precious young man of God, as are his brothers, Asher and Colby.

God willing, he will be a loving, nurturing parent, as are his parents, Cory and Amelia.`

Who is Cory Ryan?

Cory is my son.

He is a Belmont-trained nationally recognized singer/songwriter.

He has served at churches, mega, modest and micro, as Director of Modern Worship.

His original music is played around the world.

He leads worship with prayer set to music.

He leads his family and friends to and through God's love and grace.

Cory is a wise man of vision, with the ability to articulate and lead.

He is trusted because he is trustworthy.

www.ingramcontent.com/pod-product-compliance
Lightning Source LLC
Chambersburg PA
CBHW071228090426
42736CB00014B/3013